QUOTATIONS SELECTED BY HELEN EXLEY
ILLUSTRATED BY ANGELA KERR

Printed simultaneously in 2002 by Exley Publications Ltd
in Great Britain and Exley Publications LLC in the USA.

12 11 10 9 8 7 6 5 4 3

ISBN 1-86187-306-9

Printed in China.

**Exley Publications Ltd, 16 Chalk Hill, Watford,
Herts WD19 4BG, UK.
Exley Publications LLC, 185 Main Street,
Spencer, MA 01562, USA.
www.helenexleygiftbooks.com**

Acknowledgements: The publishers are grateful for permission to
reproduce copyright material. Whilst every reasonable effort has
been made to trace copyright holders, the publishers would be
pleased to hear from any not here acknowledged. KENNETH
ALLSOP: Reproduced from *Letters to His Daughter* by Kenneth Allsop
(Copyright © The Estate of Kenneth Allsop 1974) by permission of
PFD on behalf of the Estate of Kenneth Allsop. THICH NHAT
HANH: Reprinted from *Being Peace* (1987) by Thich Nhat Hanh
with permission of Parallax Press, Berkeley, California. PAM
BROWN, STUART & LINDA MACFARLANE: published with
permission © Helen Exley 2002.

BE WHAT
YOU
BELIEVE IN

A HELEN EXLEY
GIFTBOOK

≡ EXLEY

Do what you believe in
and believe in what you do.
All else is a waste
of energy and time.

NISARGADATTA

*What does it matter
how one comes by the truth
so long as one pounces
upon it and lives by it.*

HENRY MILLER

Deeds, not words.

MOTTO OF
THE MCRARIE FAMILY

I am in the world to change the world.

MURIEL TUKEYSER

The one predominant duty is to find one's work and do it.

CHARLOTTE PERKINS
GILMAN

Do it! get active!!

The world is full of horror and pain, but also of compassion and commitment. If you care you can make a difference. Don't get down, get active!

DAVID BULL,
FORMER DIRECTOR OF
AMNESTY INTERNATIONAL UK

Do something.
Either lead, follow, or
get out of the way!

EDGAR J. SHALTON

The time when you
need to do something
is when no one else
is willing to do it,
when people are saying
it can't be done.

MARY FRANCES BERRY

*Go confidently
in the direction
of your dreams!
Live the life
you've imagined.*

HENRY DAVID THOREAU
(1 8 1 7 - 1 8 6 2)

A CLEAR PURPOSE

There is no road
to success but through
a clear strong purpose.
Nothing can take
its place.

THEODORE MUNGER

Before a painter puts a brush to his canvas he sees his picture mentally.... If you think of yourself in terms of a painting, what do you see? ... Is the picture one you think worth painting?

THOMAS DREIER

It is the greatest of
all mistakes to do nothing
because you can only
do a little.

SYDNEY SMITH

You are so afraid of losing
your moral sense that you
are not willing to take it
through anything more
dangerous than
a mud-puddle.

GERTRUDE STEIN,
FROM "QED" 1903

*To know what is right
and not to do it
is the worst cowardice.*

CONFUCIUS, CHINESE
PHILOSOPHER,
(C. 551-478 BC)

*All that is necessary
for the triumph of evil
is that good men
do nothing.*

EDMUND BURKE
(1729-1797)

*It's the action, not
the fruit of the action,
that's important.
You have to do the right thing.
It may not be in your power,
may not be in your time,
that there'll be any fruit.
But that doesn't mean you
stop doing the right thing.
You may never know what
results from your action.
But if you do nothing,
there will be no result.*

MAHATMA GANDHI
(1869-1948)

...*D*are to do the deed which we well know cries to be done. Let us not hesitate because of ease, or the words of people's mouths, or our own lives. Mighty causes are calling us – the freeing of women, the training of children, the putting down of hate and murder and poverty... May we find a way to meet the task.

W.E.B. DU BOIS

People, like nails,
lose their usefulness
when they lose direction
and begin to bend.

WALTER SAVAGE LANDOR

PICK SOMETHING GREAT TO DO AND DO IT NOW

If we think defeat, this is what we will get. If we are undecided, nothing will happen to us. We must just pick something great to do and do it.

MAHARISHI MAHESH YOGI,
B.1917

You don't get to choose how you're going to die. Or when. You can only decide how you're going to live. Now.

JOAN BAEZ

... if now is not the time to act, when will it be?

HILLEL

Can anything be sadder than work unfinished? Yes; work never begun.

CHRISTINA ROSSETTI

DARE TO TRY...

Nothing great
was ever achieved
without enthusiasm.
The way of life is wonderful;
it is by abandonment.

RALPH WALDO EMERSON
(1803-1882)

Dare to be naive.

R. BUCKMINSTER FULLER

*Dreams pass into
the reality of action.
From the action stems
the dream again
and the interdependence
produces the higher form
of living.*

ANAÏS NIN
(1903-1977)

*Unless you give
yourself
to some great cause,
you haven't even
begun to live.*

WILLIAM P. MERRILL

*Our plans miscarry
because they have no aim.
When you do not know
what harbour you are
making for, no wind
is the right wind.*

MARCUS ANNAEUS SENECA

I am only one,
But still I am one.
I cannot do everything,
But still I can do something;
and because I cannot do
everything I will not refuse
to do the something that
I can do.

EDWARD E. HALE
(1822-1909)

If you think you are too small to be effective, you have never been in bed with a mosquito.

ANITA RODDICK

'Tis better to be alone than in bad company.

GEORGE WASHINGTON
(1732-1799)

The test of courage comes when we are in the minority.

RALPH W. SOCKMAN

TOTAL COMMITMENT

*If you don't make
a total commitment
to whatever you're doing,
then you start looking
to bail out the first time
the boat starts leaking.
It's tough enough*

getting that boat to shore
with everybody rowing,
let alone
when a guy stands up
and starts putting
his life jacket on.

LOU HOLTZ

*T*hings get better
when enough people
decide that they should
get better.
Things change when
ordinary people
come together in a
common purpose.

KOFI ANNAN,
SECRETARY-GENERAL
OF THE UNITED NATIONS,
1999

SPEAK OUT!

*When we have the courage
to speak out – to break
our silence – we inspire
the rest of the "moderates"
in our communities
to speak up and to vote
their views.*

SHARON SCHUSTER

$\mathcal{V}$icious prejudice,
indifference, cruelty,
the misuse of other creatures
to serve our greed and
vanity, is rife as ever.
But now, at long, long last,
we ordinary people have
a voice. We cannot be
silenced by mockery
or force. We recognise
the wrongs and so can
begin to put them right.

PAM BROWN, B.1928

*Do not follow where
the path may lead.
Go instead where there is
no path and leave a trail.*

AUTHOR UNKNOWN

*The man with courage
is a majority.*

ANDREW JACKSON
(1 7 6 7 - 1 8 4 5)

*Progress results only
from the fact
that there are some men
and women who refuse
to believe that
what they know to be right
cannot be done.*

RUSSELL W. DAVENPORT

COURAGE FOR
A GREAT CAUSE

You gain strength,
courage, and confidence
by every experience
in which you really stop
to look fear in the face.
You are able to say
to yourself, "I lived through
this horror. I can take
the next thing
that comes along."

ELEANOR ROOSEVELT
(1884-1962)

*Remember all courage
is not in fighting.
Constancy in a good cause
being the chief.*

CHARLES I

It is not by going out for a demonstration against nuclear missiles that we can bring about peace. It is with our capacity of smiling, breathing, and being at peace.

THICH NHAT HANH,
FROM "SUFFERING IS NOT
ENOUGH"

*It's not what you do
once in awhile, it's what
you do day in and day out
that makes the difference.*

JENNY CRAIG

*I believe that all of us
have the capacity for
one adventure inside us,
but great adventure
is facing responsibility
day after day.*

WILLIAM GORDON,
EPISCOPAL BISHOP
OF ALASKA

When you really believe
in what you're doing,
you must persevere despite
all obstacles.

LEE IACOCCA

*Good things are not done
in a hurry.*

GERMAN APHORISM

*The successful are the people
who have fallen flat
a dozen times – but have
got to their feet again.*

PAM BROWN, B.1928

*The whole thing is about
earning your own way and
you don't really get there
until you earn it.
That's the real truth.*

TINA TURNER

To do anything in this world worth doing, we must not stand back shivering and thinking of the cold and the danger, but jump in and scramble through as well as we can.

SYDNEY SMITH

We must dare, and dare again, and go on daring.

GEORGES JACQUES DANTON

A life spent in making mistakes is not only more honourable, but more useful than a life spent doing nothing.

GEORGE BERNARD SHAW
(1 8 5 6 - 1 9 5 0)

A SOLO VOYAGE

*The ability to pursue
a course, whether it is
a popular one or not,
is measured in courage.
The greater the courage,
the greater the possibility
we will act for change.*

MILDRED PITTS WALTER,
FROM
"THE HORN BOOK"

Whatever course you decide upon, there is always someone to tell you that you are wrong. There are always difficulties arising which tempt you to believe that your critics are right. To map out a course of action and follow it to an end requires courage.

RALPH WALDO EMERSON
(1803-1882)

A LIFE OF SERVICE

No need for witty words
or brave deeds –
just being there, when

times are tough,
is often all that's needed.

STUART AND LINDA
MACFARLANE

*It's doing small things
for the love of each other –
just a smile, or carrying
a bucket of water,
or showing some simple
kindness....
It's not how much we give,
but how much love
we put in the doing...*

MOTHER TERESA
(1910-1997)

KINDNESS SPREADS OUT

*We can as individuals do so
little to help the suffering in
the world – the lonely,
bereaved, imprisoned,
despised, exiled, the cold,
the hungry.
Yet we can reach out to
those within our knowledge,
with courtesy and kindness,
an unexpected gift, a visit.*

*Treating them with the
respect that they deserve.
Honouring their courage.
Listening to their stories.
Accepting them as kin,
as friends.
For every kindness spreads
in a shining circle – See how
good people everywhere set
rings of light moving across
the darkness, rings that link
and interlock and keep at bay
the forces of the night.*

PAM BROWN, B.1928

To awaken each morning
with a smile brightening
my face; to greet the day
with reverence for the
opportunities it contains;
to approach my work with
a clean mind; to hold ever
before me, even in the
doing of little things,
the ultimate purpose
toward which I am working;
to meet men and women
with laughter on my lips

*and love in my heart;
to be gentle, kind,
and courteous through all
the hours; to approach the
night with weariness that
ever woos sleep and the joy
that comes from work well
done this is how I desire to
waste wisely my days.*

THOMAS DEKKER
(C . 1 5 7 0 - 1 6 4 1)

*I long to accomplish a
great and noble task,
but it is my chief duty to
accomplish small tasks, as
if they were great and noble.*

HELEN KELLER
(1880-1968)

*Try not to become
someone of success.
Rather become a person
of value.*

ALBERT EINSTEIN
(1879-1955)

*We must not, in trying to
think of how we can make
a big difference ignore
the small daily differences
we can make which, over
time, add up to big
differences that we often
cannot forsee.*

MARIAN WRIGHT EDELMAN

TRUE SUCCESS

*A person's true wealth
is the good he or she does
in the world.*

MOHAMMED

*I'd rather have roses
on my table than diamonds
on my neck.*

EMMA GOLDMAN
(1869-1940)

When you look back
on your life and count
your blessings
these will not be reckoned
in terms of money
accumulated or rank
achieved. Instead
what will prove to be
most important are
the deeds you have done
for others.

STUART AND LINDA
MACFARLANE

What is at the summit of courage, I think, is freedom. The freedom that comes with the knowledge that no earthly power can break you; that an unbroken spirit is the only thing you cannot live without; that in the end it is the courage of conviction that moves things, that makes all change possible.

PAULA GIDDINGS

*It takes courage for a person
to listen to his own goodness
and act on it.*

GAUTAMA SIDDARTHA
(C.563–C.483 BC)

... there are no short cuts you have to work for what is worth having. But also, and this is much more important, it's in the work that the most satisfactions lie the satisfaction of stretching yourself, using your abilities and making them expand and knowing that you have accomplished something that could have been done

only by you using your unique apparatus. This really is at the centre of life, and those who never orientate themselves in this direction are missing more than they ever know.

KENNETH ALLSOP,
IN A LETTER
TO HIS DAUGHTER

ORDINARY PEOPLE CHANGING THE WORLD

We must remember that one determined person can make a significant difference, and that a small group of determined people can change the course of history.

SONIA JOHNSON

Hope is like a road in the country; there was never a road, but when many people walk on it, the road comes into existence.

LIN YUTANG

To keep our faces toward change, and behave like free spirits, is strength undefeatable.

HELEN KELLER
(1880-1968)

Only one feat is possible: not to have run away.

DAG HAMMARSKJOLD
(1905-1961)

STRENGTH AND COURAGE

*I will not shrink from
undertaking what seems
wise and good because
I labor under the double
handicap of race and sex,
but, striving to preserve
a calm mind with
a courageous and cheerful
spirit, barring bitterness
from my heart, I will
struggle all the more
earnestly to reach the goal.*

MARY CHURCH TERRELL

*E*ach time a man stands up
for an ideal or acts to
improve the lot of others or
strikes out against injustice,
he sends forth a tiny ripple
of hope, and crossing
each other from a million
different centers of energy
and daring, those ripples
build a current that can
sweep down the mightiest
walls of oppression and
resistance.

ROBERT KENNEDY
(1925-1968)

KEEP ON MOVING

Keep on moving,
keep on insisting,
keep on fighting
injustice.

MARY CHURCH TERRELL,
IN "JOURNAL
OF NEGRO HISTORY",
JANUARY 1938

*We can do anything
we want to do
if we stick with it
long enough.*

HELEN KELLER
(1880-1968)

You can't help someone
uphill without getting
closer to the top yourself.

PROVERB

To have a purpose
that is worthwhile,
and that is steadily
being accomplished,
that is one of the secrets
of a life that is
worth living.

HERBERT GASSON

Success is knowing that because of you, the world is a little better.

MICHAEL SNEYD

To leave the world a better place

To laugh often and much;
to win the respect of
intelligent people and the
affection of children;
to earn the appreciation
of honest critics and endure
the betrayal of false friends.
To appreciate beauty;
to find the best in others;

to leave the world a bit
better whether by a healthy
child, a garden patch or a
redeemed social condition;
to know that even one life
has breathed easier
because you have lived.
This is to have succeeded.

RALPH WALDO EMERSON
(1803-1882)

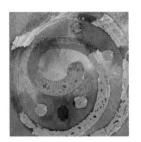

*Do continue to believe
that with your feeling and
your work you are taking
part in the greatest;
the more strongly you
cultivate in yourself
this belief, the more will
reality and the world
go forward from it.*

RAINER MARIA RILKE
(1875-1926)

*One does what one must –
in spite of personal
consequences, in spite of
obstacles and dangers
and pressures – and that is
the basis of all morality.*

JOHN F. KENNEDY

*We couldn't possibly know
where it would lead,
but we knew it had
to be done.*

BETTY FRIEDAN,
ON THE
WOMEN'S MOVEMENT

Here I stand.
I can do no other.

MARTIN LUTHER

What is a *Helen Exley Giftbook?*

Helen Exley has been creating giftbooks for twenty-six years, and her readers have bought forty-eight million copies of her works, in over thirty languages. Because her books are all bought as gifts, she spares no expense in making sure that each book is as thoughtful and meaningful a gift as it is possible to create: good to give, good to receive. The theme of personal values is very important in Helen's life, and she has now created several titles on this theme.

Team members help to find thoughtful quotations from literally hundreds of sources, and the books are then personally created. With infinite care, Helen ensures that each spread is individually designed to enhance the feeling of the words, and that the whole book has real depth and meaning.

You have the result in your hands. If you have found it valuable - tell others! We'd rather put the money into more good books than waste it on advertising when there is no power on earth like the word-of-mouth recommendation of friends.

Helen Exley Giftbooks

16 Chalk Hill,
Watford, Herts, WD19 4BG, UK

185 Main Street, Spencer,
MA 01562, USA

www.helenexleygiftbooks.com